Rex Wrecks

by

Dr. Nicholas Oeser, PsyD

Illustrated by Taryn Costello

DORRANCE
PUBLISHING CO
EST. 1920
PITTSBURGH, PENNSYLVANIA 15238

Dorrance Publishing Co
585 Alpha Drive
Suite 103
Pittsburgh, PA 15238
Visit our website at *www.dorrancebookstore.com*

ISBN: 978-1-4809-8435-6
eISBN: 978-1-4809-8454-7

For parents, therapists, and educators. The purpose of this book is for children to be able to identify with a relatable character and plot in order to reveal their own emotional states within a narrative. This book is intended to serve as a therapeutic aid for therapists, parents, and educators. More specifically, it was designed for those who are attempting to connect with children who have a history of aggressive behaviors. Children who have had difficulty expressing negative emotions may benefit by experiencing a cathartic (or emotional releasing) effect while reading with an adult helper who can provide encouragement and support.

Before reading with the child, prepare your own questions to ask the child as you read the story. Allow time for the child to think about what is being read. This could be done by a reader being aware of the child's emotions, and asking question like "What is Rex doing here?" or "What do you think Rex is feeling when _____?" This can include simply being aware and curious of the child's emotional presentation ("smiling, sad, angry, etc."). Questions, answers, and observations should be reviewed with the child after the story is completed. Enjoy!

Rex Wrecks

Meet Rex.

He is a dinosaur that enjoys
playing and learning new things.

One day Rex saw a terrible thing
that scared him very much.

He pretended the thing did not happen,
but the bad feelings would not go away.

He got angry. He would kick, hit,
and even bite the other dinosaurs.

He even pushed his teacher, Mrs. Saratops!

He kept getting into trouble,
which made him feel worse.

Rex went to see a helping dinosaur, named Dr. Steg.
This made him angry!

After some time, Rex felt safe with Dr. Steg
and enjoyed coming to see him.

To show Dr. Steg what scared him,
Rex played with the toys in the office.

Rex looked at Steg, who had a sad and scared face. He said, "Rex, what you saw would make any dino, even adult dinosaurs, angry or sad. But what happened is not your fault."

Dr. Steg gave examples of emotions
that can show other dinos the way Rex felt.

Rex felt better learning that it is okay
to have big feelings, good and bad types.

Rex practiced showing his feelings with Steg,
his parents, friends, and Mrs. Saratops.

In the end he stopped seeing Steg, since Rex learned how to practice the many feeling faces and tail wiggles.

Rex no longer felt a need to wreck because he wanted to have friends. He also felt happy in continuing to learn how to show feelings with everyone around him.

Follow-up

Be sure to reflect upon the reading with the child. Ask the specific questions that relate to the unique ways the child responds to the story. For example:

> "What did you learn about Rex?"
> "Has anything like this ever happened to you?"
> "I noticed on this page (display page to child), you ____."
> "How did it feel when we read this [book/page]?"

Another way to follow up with the child is have them summarize the story. Again, the goal of this book is to help the child pull affective states from this book into their own life story or narrative. Beyond asking questions, depending on the child's developmental age, they may respond better to activities. Example activities include: "Find the [emotional state, i.e. angry] dinosaur" and "Create your own dino story." Be sure you are creative and specific toward the child.

About the Author

Nicholas Oeser is a licensed psychologist who works with children in the San Francisco Bay Area. He has worked with children and families for over ten years. He lives in Richmond, California, and enjoys hiking and spending time with his family: wife Cody and dog Tucker.